T0195664

SAY YES TO YOURSELF

You Do Not Need to Pair Up

LORETTA M. CALVERT, JD

Author of *What the Good Student Said*
and *Say Yes to Yourself Workbook*

BALBOA.PRESS

A DIVISION OF HAY HOUSE

Copyright © 2021 Loretta M. Calvert, JD.

All rights reserved. No part of this book may be used or reproduced by
any means, graphic, electronic, or mechanical, including photocopying,
recording, taping or by any information storage retrieval system
without the written permission of the author except in the case of
brief quotations embodied in critical articles and reviews.

This book is a work of non-fiction. Unless otherwise noted, the author
and the publisher make no explicit guarantees as to the accuracy of
the information contained in this book and in some cases, names of
people and places have been altered to protect their privacy.

Balboa Press books may be ordered through booksellers or by contacting:

Balboa Press
A Division of Hay House
1663 Liberty Drive
Bloomington, IN 47403
www.balboapress.com
844-682-1282

Because of the dynamic nature of the Internet, any web addresses or
links contained in this book may have changed since publication and
may no longer be valid. The views expressed in this work are solely those
of the author and do not necessarily reflect the views of the publisher,
and the publisher hereby disclaims any responsibility for them.

The author of this book does not dispense medical advice or prescribe the use
of any technique as a form of treatment for physical, emotional, or medical
problems without the advice of a physician, either directly or indirectly. The
intent of the author is only to offer information of a general nature to help you
in your quest for emotional and spiritual well-being. In the event you use any
of the information in this book for yourself, which is your constitutional right,
the author and the publisher assume no responsibility for your actions.

Any people depicted in stock imagery provided by Getty Images are
models, and such images are being used for illustrative purposes only.
Certain stock imagery © Getty Images.

Print information available on the last page.

ISBN: 978-1-9822-7204-3 (sc)
ISBN: 978-1-9822-7205-0 (e)

Library of Congress Control Number: 2021918787

Balboa Press rev. date: 09/20/2021

This book is for all the single people
who used to cry on Saturday nights.
You do not need to put a ring on it.

Contents

Preface

TWENTY-YEAR-OLD ME WAS CUTE, SMART, ADVENTUROUS, and highly in demand; however, I did not see myself that way. I suffered from low self-esteem due to a rough childhood. I married a grandiose narcissist during a low point in my life. I will not go there, because that is a different story for a different day. This book is about what I did after that marriage ended. Whom did I date? Why? What lessons can you learn from my mistakes and the mistakes of these dates?

I've changed the names to protect people, and I've also modified some jobs and other identifiers, but you will get the idea. I live in the town next to Taylor Swift's point of origin, so I may have learned a thing or two about using pain to create something. I will not start with the first person I dated. I think I need to save the best for last, so let's start somewhere else. Besides, I live in a small town; I would not want to hurt anyone's feelings. The purpose of the book is to save you time and energy.

1

Set Boundaries

PATIO FURNITURE GUY AND I MET ONLINE. HE WAS more than six feet tall, boasted military service, had dark hair and light eyes, and was a Libra. His photos showed an attractive, confident, fun-loving person who could clean up when he wanted to do so for an occasion. We started talking through Facebook. Eventually, we exchanged numbers to have real phone calls. I could hear his voice, and he could establish that he was not being catfished. "You are too good to be true, girl," he said. He told me about one of the other females in my age range in our town. I had seen her photo too and thought it had to be a meme. No one would post a photo of herself missing teeth and using a beer can as a hair roller.

After a marriage in which I had been mostly ignored, Patio Furniture Guy's attention was sweet. He loved to text in the morning, at lunch, and to say good night, even if we had talked for an hour that day. He would hear a song, think of me, and then send me a YouTube link to the song. I would listen and reciprocate. We went back and forth like that for a while. It was also during the COVID-19 pandemic, so everyone had too much time on his or her hands. After bumping into some people online who would text and then disappear when I made it clear I was not looking for a casual hookup, I enjoyed Patio Furniture Guy's enthusiasm and outlook.

We met one day in a parking lot for breakfast. The first thing I noticed was that he did not use current photos. Patio Furniture Guy was much skinnier and had all gray hair on his head. I wondered, *How old were those photographs he used?* However, he was all smiles, polite, and easy to talk to; plus, he shared my love of music. A successful breakfast meant he graduated to a lunch date.

He met my friend Mary when I had to stop by my office. "He seems sane," she said. "But if you go missing, I can describe him to the police. Good luck."

Eventually, Patio Furniture Guy and I did dinner and a movie together. At that point, even though we were dating, the texting leveled up. I was getting about one hundred texts a day, from the minute my phone was turned on to when I shut it down at night.

We had been dating for two weeks when he introduced me to his younger son, who was around nineteen. Then he wanted me to meet his older son, wanted to plan vacations together, and started complaining about his apartment lease being up soon. Then he told me he loved me.

You, dear reader, have probably realized already what I did not: he was a narcissist. He was love-bombing me.

Once I saw the red flags, I could not unsee them. I decided to set a boundary. The boundary was for him to stop texting me during work hours. My job had started up again with masks and social distancing. I did not have time for so many texts.

He did not respect the boundary.

When I ended the relationship, I calmly explained that I had made a request and that he had not respected it. "You didn't listen to me, Patio Furniture Guy."

There is a thing called narcissistic rage, and that was what he displayed. The last words he said were "Oh, I listen. I'll show you."

Click.

I had divorced a narcissist, so this person did not scare me. I am also an excellent shot and have guns strategically placed in my home.

I went to bed. The next morning, as I was getting ready for work, I swore I heard something outside my door. I presumed it was my neighbor leaving for her job. I opened my door at seven fifteen to head to my car. I found patio furniture waiting for me on my doorstep.

During one of my conversations with Patio Furniture Guy, I had mentioned I had ordered two chairs, but the order had been canceled due to COVID-19 shortages. The chairs on my doorstep were the exact chairs I'd mentioned but in a different color. He was trying to show me he listened. I thought sarcastically, *No, that's not odd at all.* I put down my coffee and briefcase to move the furniture inside and then left for work.

He texted me a few weeks later. Patio Furniture Guy wanted me to know how great he was doing and that he still thought of me. He never mentioned the chairs, but we both knew. Weird. I never sat in those chairs. I couldn't bring myself to do it.

TAKEAWAYS

The odds that I would leave a narcissist only to find another narcissist are actually pretty good. If you believe in law-of-attraction theory, then like attracts like. Dysfunction will find dysfunction. In addition, narcissism is on the rise. There are more narcs out there than ever before, so do your research, and know the signs. I have found videos on YouTube from Dr. Ramani and Lisa A. Romano helpful on breaking down warning signs.

Also, set boundaries, and stick to them. Your boundaries define who you are and how you want to be treated. Consciously make the effort to define what you want in a relationship before setting out for a mate. You need to enforce the boundaries, though; otherwise, well, you'll see.

2

Do Not Give Second Chances

Mr. Ex-Chippendale Dancer was a blue-collar guy who owned his own drywall business. He also liked to brag, saying, for example, "I did this country singer's kitchen," "I know that athlete," or "I was in that producer's in-home recording studio." I walked away from the big talk. People like that are a dime a dozen. However, he did something that caught my eye when I first saw him at a party I attended: dance. He was the only one dancing, and he did not care he was alone while shaking his moneymaker.

I have loved to dance since I can remember being upright and walking on two legs. I begged for dance lessons as a child, but my parents couldn't afford them. I learned my moves by watching others and being my creative, badass self. I usually was the one at parties to start the dancing, and guys might shyly follow.

Ex-Chippendale Dancer did not give a hoot what anyone else was doing; he went with the music. He had rhythm. When he asked some of the women at the party to dance and kept getting turned down, I stepped up and said yes. He asked me out that night, and I said yes to that also.

Ex-Chippendale Dancer had my number, and he knew where I lived, yet he did not call. He had had a lot to drink when we met. The possibility crossed my mind that when he'd woken up the next morning, he had not remembered who I was. I even bumped into him one day while he was walking his dog. I waved and got duck-the-head-and-run body language. Maybe he was ashamed of how drunk he had been, I thought, but it had been a fun night.

A couple of weeks passed, and a friend invited me to another party. There was Ex-Chippendale Dancer. I saw it clearly this time: he was a happy drunk who wanted to dance, eat, tell dirty jokes, and brag. He reminded me of an overly eager Irish setter. We danced again. He asked me out again. I said yes again.

Then I did not hear from him again.

I asked my friend who had organized the parties, "What is Ex-Chippendale Dancer's deal?"

Yolanda gave me a big grin, took a puff of her cigarette, and tapped her phone. The pictures that popped up were stuff no one would want on the internet. Apparently, Ex-Chippendale Dancer was tabloid-level crazy when he drank and often did not remember stuff he said or did. This man who owned a successful business never had learned not to let someone take naked pictures of him. Yolanda said, "Don't count on him."

Ex-Chippendale Dancer was generous and witty, but he was not someone to date. Message received.

TAKEAWAYS

Do not give people second, third, or fourth chances. Adult men know how to follow through when setting a date. In addition, if they need to be drunk to ask you out, they probably have low self-esteem.

People will show you who they really are—believe them. Don't select a fixer-upper. You deserve a man, not a little boy who doesn't have his shit together.

3

Trust Your Gut

Mr. Future Dateline Story was another online match. He was a good-looking person, athletic, and funny. Future *Dateline* Story also wasted no time. We exchanged numbers to start talking offline. He asked me out, and he started making plans.

Future *Dateline* Story was different from the others right away. Future *Dateline* Story wanted to take me for a hike. Now, why my brain instantly went to every episode of *Dateline* that involved serial killers, I do not know, but once I got that idea, I could not shake it. I picked the trail we would do. I appreciated doing something different from dinner and a movie. However, I was meeting someone I did not know on a trail where he could kill me and dump my body in the trees. I debated going through with the date but decided I would have a concealed knife for protection and my cell phone. I had two friends who knew my plans and checked on me.

Off I went one sunny Saturday morning to meet Future *Dateline* Story, the potential serial killer. I arrived first and sent the girls a text: "Maybe he won't show up."

He arrived, and he looked exactly like his pictures. Future *Dateline* Story was tall, good looking, and built and had a huge smile on his face.

"He's here. Wish me luck," I texted to my friends.

Future *Dateline* Story and I did the trail. He was smart and funny. He seemed to enjoy nature. Although Future *Dateline* Story was from the area, he claimed not to know the trail or any of the surrounding neighborhoods and stores. I took photos along the hike and posted them, remembering the two young girls who had disappeared in one of the *Dateline* episodes.

After the hike, he asked about places to eat lunch. Future *Dateline* Story followed me to a nearby eatery. When he looked over the menu, he commented that he hardly ever ate out, because he was careful about what he put into his body. I could tell he took care of himself, except for his hands. I had not noticed it on the hike, but as we looked over our menus, I realized his hands were covered in weird markings. File that away for later.

We ordered. Future *Dateline* Story told me about all the amazing meals he made and said he cooked with fresh items from his garden. He told me he would love to cook for me. *Cook me or cook for me?* I wondered. He graciously paid the bill.

At that point, it was around two o'clock in the afternoon and still light out. Future *Dateline* Story asked if I wanted to go for a ride to a local park. "Okay, sure," I said. I had been texting the girls on and off, letting them know where I was, so I had my security plan in place. I checked my knife, and it was still there. I climbed into his truck, and off we went.

He took me to his favorite park. *So you do know the area*, I thought. We chatted and enjoyed the fresh air. We watched a person fly his model airplanes at the park. There were dogs and birds to watch also.

Future *Dateline* Story kissed me, and he was a good kisser. He had strong arms. He probably had less than 10 percent body fat. However, instead of thinking about how lucky I was, the thought crossed my mind that he could easily snap my neck.

We climbed into his truck. I asked to go back.

"One last stop before I take you back. It's still early," he said as he slipped his hand into mine. He was right—it was still early—but I started to get the Spidey sense. I texted the girls names of roads as we drove.

We ended up pulling up to his house. He said, "I want to show you my garden."

Future *Dateline* Story was proud of his garden, and he had every right to be. The yard was a lush green and had all sorts of vegetables, herbs, and wildlife. He asked me if I wanted to go inside.

I said, "No, thank you. Another time. I really need to get back home."

"You sure you don't want to stay and go inside? I can make us dinner tonight."

First, there was no way I wanted a first date to last from ten o'clock in the morning until dinnertime or longer. Second, I didn't know him. I was getting a spooky, creeped-out feeling as the sun started to set.

"Next time," I said with a smile.

We got back in the truck. On the ride back, he held and kissed my hand; however, he also did this weird licking thing. He might have been trying to simulate oral sex on my hand. *Insert raised eyebrow.*

In the parking lot, next to my car, he kissed me again. He was a good kisser, but as he waved, I caught another good look at the markings on his hands. Gardening or defensive wounds from his last kill? You decide. I was going home.

TAKEAWAYS

Always go into a date with a set start and end time for the date. It helps you mentally because you know what level of commitment you are making. There is a difference between two hours and the entire day. I enjoy flexibility and spontaneity, but at the beginning, set times. It is important to see in the beginning if the person shows up when he or she agrees to or if he or she is late. You do not want someone who is always late. Lateness shows a lack of respect. The end time is important also because your time is valuable. If you have zero plans outside of that person, that might send an inaccurate message of your worth to a new person.

Notice Future *Dateline* Story was testing boundaries, getting me closer and closer to his house, which was where he wanted me all along. Remember your boundaries, and stick to them. Also, my gut told me something was off. Future *Dateline* Story could be a great person, but my gut told me he was not right for me and sent me signals to let me know. Our primitive fight-or-flight instinct has kept us alive for thousands of years. Listen to your gut, and stay safe by mentally knowing what in your bag can be used as a weapon.

Finally, if a person starts counting your calories at lunch, walk away.

4

Dating Apps Are for Sex

MR. NOT-SO-MODEL FATHER WAS AN ACCOUNTANT AND had three daughters. I had a theory that if a man had daughters, he would be more respectful of women. God, I was so wrong!

Not-So-Model Father was from Ecuador and fit the definition of tall, dark, and handsome. Not my usual blue- or green-eyed guy, but hey, personality and a job are good boxes to check.

We met on a dating app. Mistake! Do not use dating apps if you want a serious relationship. Dating apps, no matter what they advertise, are used strictly for hookups. I thought only Tinder was all about sex, but no, they all are. I did not know that at the time, though, so I fell for the marketing that the app I was using was a different breed of app.

I was new to dating in this century and gullible. I believed when people posted pictures, they were recent pictures. I believed when people put an age, that was their real age. I put down hobbies I actually did, not stuff I might do one day. I never lied on my dating profiles—not about my age, my job, or my marital status. I might have fudged on my location as a safety measure. However, my love of children and dogs was true.

When I saw Not-So-Model Father had three children, I was excited. Here was a man who was proud to be a dad, with all girls, and he was outdoorsy. We flirted by text and had polite exchanges. We went to the next step and exchanged real telephone numbers to communicate off the app.

That was when things went sideways. After a normal conversation, during our next conversation, he asked if I had any funny dating stories. I told him about Patio Furniture Guy. Not-So-Model Father proceeded to tell me about the squirter he'd dated who still lived with her mom. Another woman he'd dated had a DUI and an interlock device on her car and also had had no shame about being naked when he went to pick her up for their first date.

The sex talk was ridiculously graphic and so out of character that I was too shocked to react. I wondered if he had been drinking before he called. No, he told me, he was driving to his thirteen-year-old's recital twenty miles away.

Now, honestly, I was still figuring myself out after the divorce. I had also been raised, as many women are, to be agreeable and nice. What I should have done when the graphic talk started was hang up and block him immediately.

He also told me that while married, he had what he called "sex-cations" in Latin America. He mentioned it as casually as you would tell someone you are left- or right-handed.

I laughed nervously and got off the phone as quickly as possible. If he was that graphic and free with me on the phone, what did he think would happen on our first date? Also, ew, he told me about the side effects of the medications he was on, including that he did not ejaculate. *Really, dude? TMI.*

TAKEAWAYS

When a person says anything that makes you uncomfortable, hang up, and block him or her. Blocking is your best friend. I stayed on the phone too long, wasted precious time, and heard things I never needed to hear. Also, talk on the phone before you set up a face-to-face meeting. Bad vibes travel over the phone. I also am surprised he confessed to cheating on his wife and tried to normalize it. I subscribe to the "Once a cheater, always a cheater" motto.

5

Mama's Boy

Mr. Little Prince was another internet algorithm error. On some program code, we matched. We both had teaching backgrounds, were single with no children, and loved pets and sports. Little Prince asked me out to dinner at a local steakhouse. When he rolled up to meet me there, he was listening to loud rap music. I was a little surprised because homeboy was super white and bald. He later told me he had grown up poor in the projects. I am from New York City. I have been to the projects, but I let it slide. Maybe Tennessee had projects somewhere. I do understand growing up poor, and every town has a bad part of town you do not go to after sundown. *Maybe he is legit*, I thought.

We sat in a booth, facing each other. I got a better look at him as we chatted about teaching, politics, and movies. Little Prince had a face that was attractive if he was turned to a three-quarters view. Dead-on, he was not attractive; the lines were harsh. It was so disturbing to me that I switched positions to keep the three-quarters view and not dead-on, so he kept looking cute.

The date ended—no frills—and I thought he was a decent person and good enough for a second date. We actually went out about five times, and then he started planning our life together. Our life included a trip to meet the queen.

Odd, I thought. *He wants to go to England.* Then he mentioned visiting the queen in Florida.

Finally, I asked, "Who is this queen?"

"Oh, my mother. I refer to her as 'the queen.'"

Insert sound of a record scratch across the vinyl or a tire screech under a bright red light.

"Oh, okay. How did she get that nickname, Little Prince?"

"I've always called her that."

Little bells started going off, sounding like a railroad crossing. In combination with everything else, I decided to tell him I did not think a vacation was a good idea. Everything felt rushed again. We had not made it to a month yet.

TAKEAWAYS

It is great for a person to have a relationship with his mother, but watch out for mama's boys—you know, the ones who want Mom to approve of you. And heaven forbid Mom does not give you a thumbs-up.

I never met the queen. I had no interest.

Also, overnight or weekend trips are fine but maybe after three or four months. It is easy for someone to behave and present a perfect image on the first three dates. Someone's true personality tends to come out around month three. Take your time when dating. Turtles-watching-snail-races slow is better than rushing what should be a fun and memorable part of the start of a relationship.

6

Whom You Let into Your House

I DATED AND LEARNED ABOUT DATING IN ANOTHER ERA. Before I started dating again, I asked friends and looked up some dating tips. I knew not to give people my address and let them pick me up at my home in case they were weirdos. I did not know that after a few dates, inviting them into your home to hang out was code for getting naked. The following was another date-five situation, so the man and I did not know each other that well yet. We were still being polite and feeling each other out.

I had a movie set up, made microwave popcorn, and stepped out to use the bathroom. When I came back, Mr. Naked was naked. That was bad, but there is more. I had seen small penises before and had had guys warn me, "Hey, I'm on the small size." Many guys have ideas about their size. Most, it seemed, were around three inches soft but grew to four. Mr. Naked was hard and only the size of a Jolly Rancher. I am not exaggerating—a fun-size Snickers is bigger. I had never seen a micropenis before, but it is a real medical condition and normally is treated when boys are teenagers. (I Googled it afterward, because I mean, come on.) That micropenis is burned into my brain.

I shouted at him to put his clothing on. The thought that it was the size of a baby's penis hit me, and that thought and his aggressive attitude of "I'm going to undress and spring this on you" were deal breakers.

Show's over. Get out of my house!

He never warned me or gave any indication he thought we were headed toward sex or about the micropenis. Mistake! Guys, if you have a Jolly Rancher–size penis, something smaller than or around a baby-carrot size, warn your date before the pants come off. I still see that image to this day and shiver. Gross. Single and never married at forty-five may be code for a small penis.

TAKEAWAYS

If you are invited into a woman's house, that does not mean you are getting sex. Many women are trained in cultures across the globe to be passive people-pleasers who are polite and agreeable. When we invite you in, it could be that we want to talk, play a card game, show you a signed first edition of a John Grisham novel, or give you coffee so you stay awake for your car ride home. An invite into a home does not mean sex is happening.

If sex is something your relationship is ready for, please have a discussion before the act. Hopefully you know important details about the individuals you are about to couple with. For example, when was the last time they had sex? Do they have a sexually transmitted infection? Have they ever been tested? Where do they stand on birth control? Never presume someone has the birth control taken care of and then let the energy of the moment carry you into a state in which you create an unplanned life. At one point, I had to buy my own condoms because many guys claim to have an allergy to latex or whine that you should trust them. Men do not always show symptoms of sexually transmitted diseases and infections, including HPV and trichomoniasis.

7

Mind Your Manners

MR. RUDE PICKED ME UP WHILE WE WERE WAITING IN line at a meat-and-three joint. He was not my typical person physically because he was shorter than I was, but this dude had a full head of hair, which was rare at the age I was dating. He offered to buy my lunch and to sit together. *Sure*, I thought.

Rude was new in town and trying to get his bearings. Ever the helpful good girl, I decided to keep him company; eat my free lunch; and give him some tips on where to go to find good food, good music, cheap gas, an eye doctor, a medical doctor, a mechanic, and more. I asked him where he worked. The business was a place I knew because a friend's husband worked there. Mr. Rude and I exchanged numbers.

I called my friend and said, "Hey, Cindy, do you happen to know a Mr. Rude who works at XYZ Corporation?"

"Oh yeah, he moved here from Alabama."

So his story checked out in terms of being new and getting settled into a new place. Cindy and I discussed how I had met Rude. After I told her, she said, "Oh, that is so cute. Are you going to go out with him?"

Because it seemed we had a mutual friend through his job, I suggested a double date.

Friday night, Rude and I were in one restaurant, and my friend and her husband were at a Halloween party at a different restaurant. There had been a miscommunication on the dates and locations.

Rude and I were at a place with live music he was enjoying. Cindy sent me a text: "Come meet us."

Too late now! Rude and I had ordered drinks. The band playing was good and taking requests, so we stayed. I was enjoying myself too, but the band was so loud we couldn't talk.

As we sat there, I watched him drink beer after beer. He shouted at me, "Are you having a good time?"

I shouted back, "Yes!" Honestly, I was not at that point, but I could tell he was loving it. My free lunch did not feel so free right then.

"Do you want another drink?" he asked.

"No," I said, shaking my head, because I was going deaf at that point.

I was the driver and was not interested in getting a DUI. I was the one driving and showing him around. He ordered another drink and another.

I get it. Men can drink a six-pack of beer and think they are fine to drive, and depending on size, they might be okay. I had one drink, and I was the designated driver. I was ready to leave when the band took a break before the third set.

Rude said, "You're a party pooper."

I filed that away in my brain. The bill arrived, and he graciously paid, but I noticed he tipped only 10 percent. The poor young girl who'd brought over all those beers and whoever had to carry away those bottles would get only 10 percent.

TAKEAWAYS

Maybe do not drink so much on a first date. It can send the wrong impression. In addition, it can make you say stupid things, such as calling your date a party pooper. I was being responsible. Do not tease, make digs, or insult your date or how your date drives. You don't know each other yet. This is not the time for sarcastic comments.

When you tip in the United States, follow the rules on tipping. In certain situations, a 10 percent tip is fine, but in others, give 15, 18 for great service, and 20 for an amazing waitstaff. Being stingy on a date is not a good sign. It could mean stinginess in other areas, if you know what I mean. By the way, the saying "There is no such thing as a free lunch" is true.

8

Cleanliness Matters

DIRTY BOY WORKED IN SALES. HE HAD AN AMAZING smile and personality. I could understand why he had ended up in that job. Anyone who'd met him would have wanted to buy from him. Dirty Boy had charm. He was built and crazy tan and had teeth as white as Chiclets gum. I met Dirty Boy because he lived in the same apartment complex I did. He had been divorced for ten years and was in the process of having a new place built. Dirty Boy and I chatted when we bumped into each other, and eventually, he asked me out.

After a few successful dates, I went back to his apartment, where we were planning on changing into our swimsuits to go for a dip before the pool closed for the night. That was when the problem came in—the apartment was a mess! Clothing piled high. Pizza boxes piled high. Weird glasses and cups all over the place. Dirty dishes in the sink.

"Bathroom's in there," he said, pointing to the guest half bath. Dirty Boy walked back to his master bedroom.

I walked into the bathroom for more messes— toothpaste, a contact lens holder, antacids, more glasses, a pair of slippers that looked as if they were twenty years old because they were so dirty. I didn't know where to set down my stuff so I could change. The only place to set my items down was the toilet seat or the floor—in other words, germs and more germs. I put down my bag that held my swimsuit, and when it brushed against the top of the toilet seat, I saw a thick layer of dust. Shaking my head, I plowed through changing and came out.

Dirty Boy was smiling and ready. "Wow, it really takes you girls forever to get ready."

Oh, good. Clichés too.

We went to the pool. I survived the grime. I imagined any germs on me being killed by the heavy dose of chlorine in the pool. However, when we sat down and he handed me a drink, I noticed for the first time how dirty his fingernails were. I could feel disgust swirl in my stomach. There was no way those hands were coming near me for anything.

TAKEAWAYS

I am not saying you need a manicure, but you should be clean when you are dating someone. Hygiene matters. Grab a washcloth, and make sure your fingernails are clean. If you want to touch someone, those hands need to be clean.

Clean hands matter, especially in the middle of a pandemic. Cleanliness was a deal breaker for me. Other people may be fine with a mess, and may all those messy people find each other. As we say in the South, "Bless his heart."

9

Is Your Date on Your Level?

HOLLYWOOD FILMS LIKE TO PEDDLE BULL THAT OPPOSITES attract. In a movie, a millionaire can fall for a hooker. No. In real life, the millionaire ends up human-trafficking the hooker. Your date needs to be on the same level as you. For example, think about the imbalance in the relationship if you are an attorney and you date a person who works for the Geek Squad. Nothing against all those geeks out there. I consider myself a geek.

Mr. No Motivation had attended about two years of college, but I am not sure he ever got his degree. He was cute. No Motivation had a messy mop of brown curls on top of his head and brown puppy-dog eyes with the longest lashes I have ever seen that were real.

We had been on three dates and made it to date four, when I invited him over to my house for dinner on a Sunday night. I love making huge quantities of pasta with meat sauce or lasagna. No Motivation and I ate, watched a movie, and played Scrabble.

Tomorrow was a workday. I said, "It's getting late."

He did not get it.

"No Motivation, I have work to do. I need to be ready for court tomorrow."

He didn't take the hint and make his exit. I finally pulled out my laptop and files and started working in front of him.

I don't know if he thought something was supposed to happen or if he was trying to sleep over. I thought I had been clear. Finally, after twenty minutes of my typing while he watched the news, No Motivation figured out he should go.

I said, "Good night." After a kiss at the door, off he went into the night.

TAKEAWAYS

Communication is important. Women, we need to be more direct. I should have told him, "Get the hell out of my house. I need to work." Maybe don't be that harsh, but hints do not work with some people. Men, I know it is hard, but sometimes you need to read the subtext. "It's getting late" should be universal for "I am ending the date."

Most of the time, No Motivation did not get how stressful my job was and why I sometimes was working until eight o'clock at night. He could not fathom a workday that did not end at 5:00 p.m. No Motivation thought if court was closed, that meant I was not working. We might have been able to discuss the issue and negotiate some boundaries; however, he also failed to show a willingness to let go of some of his incorrect beliefs about women and work.

When I told him I didn't want to see him again, he mentioned how rude I had been that Sunday night.

I said, "Really? Me? The person who invited you over, fed you, did dishes, and spent three hours with you? I'm rude for doing my work for Monday morning?"

"Yeah, boring and rude."

I suppose it depends on perspective; however, I was done. Next, please.

10

Are You Healthy?

MR. POTENTIAL HEART ATTACK STARTED OUT AS THE perfect date. He was on time in picking me up. He brought me a bouquet of flowers. In our conversations, he showed he was self-reflective, had a steady job he was passionate about, and was kind to others. He was also six years younger than I was and never had been married. Potential Heart Attack had come close to marriage a couple of times. His last fiancée had two kids, and he said the breakup had not been anyone's fault.

I invited him into my home after dinner ended. We sat down on the living room couch to watch a movie. Halfway through the movie, we started kissing, but there was no *zing* for me.

Suddenly, he backed away and started wheezing. Potential Heart Attack stood up. His face was red, and drops of sweat fell from his forehead.

I cocked my head to the side and asked, "You okay?"

"I feel bad," he said with a hand on his chest.

"Don't feel bad. It's fine. Should I open a window?"

"No, I feel bad. I need to go to the ER."

Shocked, I jumped off the couch and into action. I went to find my shoes and car keys; however, I was blocked in by his car. I said, "Hey, I'll need to drive your car."

"Yeah, yeah. You ready, Loretta?"

We got in his car and headed the two miles to the hospital. On the way, he called someone. "Ma, I'm going to the emergency room." He turned to me. "Loretta, what's the name of it?"

I gave the name and directions to the hospital for his mother; however, I also wondered why he was calling his mom. He did not call a sibling, a friend, or even his dad. Potential Heart Attack called his mother. *Oh no, I am going to meet his mom like this*, I thought.

We got to the hospital. I dropped him off at the door, parked the car, and walked inside. Potential Heart Attack was filling out paperwork. We soon were back in a room after a few questions, and the male nurse and doctor hooked him up to machines. I would have been fine to stay in the waiting room, but the staff had me come back with him. I answered questions while he changed into a hospital gown.

"What were you doing when this started?"

Not that! I think.

The nurse and doctor asked what we'd had for dinner, what medications he took, and what his first symptom had been. I was hearing way too much personal information, and his mom was on her way. I needed an escape plan.

Early in the dating process, my friend Marie told me, "If you ever get stranded and need a ride, call me." I sent her a text message. Faithful Marie came to my rescue in her pajamas. I extricated myself like Tom Cruise in *Mission Impossible*.

TAKEAWAYS

Everyone needs a friend like Marie. Who are you going to call if you and your date have a fight and he is a jerk who leaves you at the movie theater? My friends were valuable assets when I was dating. Marie saved me from having my date's mother drive me home. I will never forget that act of kindness.

Also, I hope you already know this, but continue to see your friends. I never disappeared from my friends' lives when I was dating. Keep your life intact, and avoid becoming totally enmeshed in your new prospect.

11

Is This a Date?

Twice now, I have been in a situation in which one of my male friends suggested meeting, and I was unclear if it was a date or not. Let me give you both circumstances so you can see how easy it is for things to get confusing.

Mr. Video Game was a new friend. We'd met during a trivia night organized by three mutual friends. Actually, we had won trivia night the first time too. I love money prizes.

Well, Video Game and I decided to hang out one night without the group. I didn't even think about whether it was a date or not, because I thought we were only friends. We went out for sushi and then went back to his house to play video games. (Yes, at my age, I still play on a PlayStation.) It got dark, and then I went home.

The next time I saw two of our mutual friends, I told them I had seen Video Game.

"What do you mean you saw him? Like a date?"

"No. We had dinner and then hung out."

"That is a date, Loretta."

"No, we were hanging out as friends."

"Loretta, where did you go?"

"Sushi."

"Did he pay?"

"Yeah."

They looked at each other and, at the same time, said, "It was a date."

"Oh."

I didn't know what I thought about that, because I was new to that friend group. I firmly believe in being direct and to the point. The next time I saw Video Game, I asked him if it had been a date. He said, "I don't know."

Oh, good, I thought. *It's not just me who is confused.*

We talked it out and laughed. It was not a date; we were only friends.

Mr. Friend Zone and I had worked for the same employer. He knew my ex-spouse and the roller coaster I had been on. However, one night, he asked me to a fancy Italian restaurant, the sort of place that has cloth napkins and requires reservations.

Odd, I thought. Then it occurred to me: *Could this be a date?* Suddenly, tried and true Friend Zone took on a different hue. Could we make the move from friends to something more?

Well, he did not pick me up. We met there. The dinner was delicious and filling. We ordered dessert. The bill came, and he handed it to me.

I looked at him as if he had sprouted six heads. "What's up?"

"It's your turn to pay," he said.

"Really? How do you figure that?" I thought about the timeline of events. He'd called me. He'd asked me to go to dinner with him. He'd picked the restaurant. He'd made the reservation.

"Yeah, I paid for Indian the last time, so it's your turn to pay."

Aha! I realized that in the friend scheme of things, he was right. I was annoyed, though. That place was not cheap, and I had sort of gotten my hopes up a little bit. I would never invite a friend to an expensive restaurant and then make him pay for my meal.

I was upset for a month, but in the end, I realized the friendship was more important.

TAKEAWAYS

Communication is vital. Unless someone says, "This is a date," then it is not a date. Also, if someone friend-zones you, then you are never getting out of that friend zone.

12

Where Is His Ex?

Doppelgänger Date was a big person with a big heart. His kindness was what piqued my interest. He had dark hair and dark eyes and was wearing denim and boots when he climbed out of his red F-150 truck. Our first date was at a local steakhouse. He was polite and funny. Having grown up in the area, Doppelgänger Date knew many aspects of local history. We were set to go to a nearby venue to check out some music and meet some of my friends. He turned to me as he was driving and said, "I need to make a stop first."

I nodded in agreement, thinking we would pull into an ATM or a gas station. We proceeded to drive to a residential area. *Okay*, I thought, *maybe he needs to get something at his house.*

We pulled up to a minimansion with a three-car garage, two levels, a swimming pool, and extensive landscaping. He said, "Wait here. I'll be right back." He was all smiles, and I smiled.

Yes, I thought, *he is probably getting a jacket.*

A woman opened the front door. She was my age and my height, with my hair color and my body build. She leaned in and gave him a hug. They went inside.

Sister? I wondered. *One Mississippi. Two Mississippi,* I counted, and I said to myself, "Let's see how long this takes."

The front door opened to reveal them after fifteen minutes. Doppelgänger Date walked back to the truck. The woman shot me a look that could have curdled milk. He slid into the truck, and off we went again.

"Hey, what was that about?" I asked.

"Oh, I had to drop off the child-support check. My ex needed it for the tuition."

A few things went through my head at that point. Doppelgänger Date seemed to have a type. If you'd put me and his ex side by side, there would have been no denying the doppelgänger effect. I also wondered why he had not mailed the check; used a money-transfer app, such as Venmo; or dropped it off earlier when he did not have a new woman with him.

Eventually, the thought creeped in that he was using me to send a message to his ex-wife. I swatted that thought away like a group of gnats. His delivery of the money was an act of kindness, I thought.

The rest of the night was a normal Saturday night at a bar, where we listened to live music. The noise level made it impossible to talk; however, there was the joy of bonding over our bad singing and beers while stomping our feet in time to the music.

Doppelgänger Date and I had another date, and over Thai food, I asked some questions about his ex-wife. They were close. They were coparenting his son and daughter. The divorce sounded like a situation in which two people had realized they no longer loved each other and parted ways. However, I saw a tiny bit of a red flag because I remembered the look she had given me.

The following week, I received a text two hours before our next date. Doppelgänger Date had to cancel. "I am so sorry, but my ex is having car problems. I have to go help her," he wrote.

Really? I thought. *You have to help?* I do not doubt she had car problems. I do not doubt he was only going to pick her up from wherever she was stranded. My issue was that their lives were a little too enmeshed. His ex-wife had no friends or family to call during her car crisis?

I ended up ordering delicious takeout delivered by an Uber driver, who appreciated my skirt and heels. "Honey, you are too fabulous. I love those shoes. Do you remember if they had a size twelve where you bought them?"

TAKEAWAYS

Ask about the person's last relationship when you go on your first or second date. Was he or she married? How does your date talk about the ex? Seeing an ex-spouse at the kids' soccer game is one thing. However, in Doppelgänger Date's case, seeing each other multiple times a week, having family dinners every week, and taking vacations together sounded like a little too much together time for people raising teenagers. Doppelgänger Date told me he even still mowed her lawn. Again, I do not think that was some sort of sexual innuendo, but it was a bit above and beyond the call of duty. Maybe he was even still hung up on her. Not my issue to fix, so I moved along.

13

Watch Out for Takers

MANY DATING PROFILES WANT TO KNOW YOUR occupation, and mine really gets people going. When I say I am a lawyer, most people have a strong negative reaction. Not all lawyers do personal injury or represent murderers, rapists, or large corporations who are out to screw the little person. Many attorneys are human beings who offer a service to people who are in a critical stage of their lives.

Mr. Legal Questions had been through a messy divorce and had two children with his ex-wife. I did not know that when we first started talking. At first, our conversations were about sports, work, books, and movies. Finally, after a couple of weeks of flirting online and sending text messages, we set up a Zoom call to see each other.

First, he was not prepared for the call. In fact, for the first fifteen minutes of the call, he had me on the phone and tried to talk and type notes for his job. Eventually, I said, "Do what you need to do. I'll be back."

Therefore, to kill time, I started browsing the web. He finished his notes and finally could focus. We started chatting, and things started to come out that he had glossed over in the past. I came to find out he was adopted. I came to find out about the ex-wife and their relationship struggles. Then I made the mistake of asking about his children, because I wanted to know if he had custody on weekends, as that would affect his time to date. At that point, he launched into an hour-long discussion of the custody battle. In the end, I was giving him free legal advice on things he could try if he wanted to represent himself and modify the arrangement. We had been on Zoom for almost three hours. I politely got off the call.

I chewed on the thought of my providing legal advice. That had happened before. A person who was still married but listed as single on the dating websites contacted me through a dating app. He wanted to know what to do if his wife did not agree to the divorce. Their biggest asset was the house they lived in together. I thought, *Rewind that—you are out there representing yourself as single, but you are married and even still live with your wife? No. Not interested in hearing anything else; I'm done.* Another reason not to use dating apps.

TAKEAWAYS

People who want free legal advice but can afford to pay annoy me. If your car broke down, would you expect the mechanic to fix it for free? If you needed dental work done, would you expect the dentist to do that for free too? How about when you go out to eat? Is your meal supposed to be free? You pay for all those services. Why try to get a freebie on something that is serious enough you need a lawyer involved?

If you can avoid putting your profession on a dating website, do it. If you offer a service, such as massage, physical therapy, or medical care, someone looking for free help might hit you up online.

14

Blocking Bad Juju

Mr. Potty Mouth worked at an insurance company in the town over from mine. He was in a rush from the first time we met. We matched up online, and he sent me a message immediately after I joined. Mr. Potty Mouth wanted to exchange cell phone numbers. He wanted to have lunch, have dinner, sleep over, move in together, and go on vacation together. Mr. Potty Mouth wanted a relationship, and he wanted one now.

After how quickly some men had moved, such as Patio Furniture Guy, I saw a series of red flags. Finally, there were so many red flags on the field I had to say something. Mr. Potty Mouth was nice, but he acted needy and odd. He thought nothing of coming over one night with his pillow and toothbrush. We had arranged for a dinner date.

"What the heck is all this?" I asked.

"Oh, I wanted to be comfortable."

"You are not staying the night."

"Oh, really? But I have problems driving at night. I have bad night vision."

Too bad, I thought. *Drive home slowly.*

After that, I decided I needed to tell him to slow down and needed to set boundaries before he started picking out wedding venues. I blocked him on Facebook and decided

I would talk to him that night. After the block, I instantly felt better, but that was short-lived. About an hour later, Mr. Potty Mouth called me, cursing me out.

"You blocked me? You really blocked me? I thought we had something special."

I tried to explain I felt smothered and needed some space. It had not been a month, and already things were moving too fast for me. "Please understand."

"Well, you don't block someone like that, because it means you are pissed at them. I didn't do anything wrong."

"Well, I am new to dating. I had no idea about this blocking rule, but I did plan to talk to you."

I realized later how he'd figured out I blocked him and why he was so angry. He had been with his friends and wanted to brag about the new relationship he was in. When he'd tried to show them my Facebook profile, he'd figured it out.

TAKEAWAYS

I think Mr. Potty Mouth would have been with anybody so he could tell himself and others he was in a relationship. Mr. Potty Mouth seemed not to enjoy alone time. He was extremely needy and wanted his friends to boost his self-esteem by validating him and seeing his hot girlfriend. This is not high school. I am a grown-up. He is a grown-up. He did not act like one, though. Next.

15

Your Friends Are Not Dating Him

MR. GLORY DAYS WAS SOMEONE I MET ON MY OWN IN the natural world, with no stupid dating-app algorithm, who ended up knowing my friend Anna. I was trying to break the physical type I normally went for, and Mr. Glory Days was the same height as I was. He was also not clean-shaven, which is my personal preference. I had gone on a few dates with him before Anna realized they knew each other from high school.

We decided to do a double date with Anna and her husband, Derek. The four of us met at a local pizza joint that offered a variety of beers and large-screen televisions on multiple walls. We had not been sitting for long before Anna and Glory Days started reminiscing about high school.

"Do you remember Beth?"

"I heard she married Bobby."

"I saw Chris last month. He is working at corporate now."

This went on and on for more than an hour or two.

Derek and I started watching the game on the closest television, bored to death with a conversation about people we did not know and where they were now. Glory Days also took a couple of jabs at my age because I was older than he was. I smiled at the bad jokes, but inside, my level of annoyance was doing a slow creep up from my stomach to the center of my chest. He was supposed to be a nice guy who, although he was not a looker, was going to be kind and treat me right. Guess not. I was happy when the date ended. I promised myself, *Never again.*

TAKEAWAYS

If you are on a date and your date spends most of the date talking to your friend and not you, move along. If your date pokes fun at you, check your feelings. Is that acceptable to you, or did it cross a line? My annoyance level reached my eyeballs when Anna told me the next day how excited she was that I was dating him. She said, "He would be a great addition to our group. Way more fun than Video Game."

Your friends are not dating him. You are dating him, and you are the one who will be spending alone time with him. I had a friend say once, "Never date a guy named Andy. My ex is named Andy." I am not going to take that into consideration. Sorry.

This man's facial hair was an issue. Actually, for me, it was a deal breaker, but I settled rather than sticking to my list of requirements. We kissed a few times, and I ended up with hair in my mouth. Not attractive.

Finally, never age-shame someone. I started to wonder if the comments about my age were an effort to make himself feel better, because he made other comments that seemed to indicate he thought I was out of his league, so to speak. Do not mock your date in order to feel better about yourself. That is common decency.

16

Kind Words and Kind Actions

MR. MISMATCH WORKED IN THE SCHOOL SYSTEM AND had a round face and straight brown hair. He seemed to be a good match on paper. We had things in common, so we chatted online to see where things went. Because I thought he was a good person with similar values, I agreed to a date. As he worked in the school system, his job required he interact with children. His dating profile claimed he enjoyed wine, books, movies, travel, and hiking.

On the date, I asked about his priorities in life. He listed baseball, motorcycles, and his boat. Mr. Mismatch did not mention anything connected to children. He did not mention how his job provided an important foundation for children and, therefore, the future of our community. Mr. Mismatch was not that deep. His dating profile was deep but did not match up with his words on the date. We differed on major aspects, including treating people with kindness and respect. He was not kind to the staff at the restaurant. Mr. Mismatch also placed a high value on money and high-ticket items. He loved his tech gadgets and his toys, but he was cheap. There were times when he reminded me of Dwight from *The Office* taking a two-ply roll of toilet paper and unrolling it to make two one-ply rolls.

We went out a couple more times. Eventually, we decided it was better to be friends rather than date. On more than one occasion, he came to my home, or I visited his. I was brought up with the understanding that when you go to someone's house, you bring something, such as a pie or a bottle of wine. Mr. Mismatch never reciprocated. He would never have wasted money on something as frivolous as flowers or wine. While his profile said he liked wine, it turned out he was really more of a beer man. One day I asked him, "Mismatch, did someone help you write your profile?"

"God, yeah. I had no idea what to write, so I had my sister do it."

Maybe I need to date her, I thought.

TAKEAWAYS

A person's words and actions need to match up. If a person says one thing but acts in a different way, then trust what his or her actions are telling you. People like to think of themselves in a certain way, and maybe they will reach that ideal they have of themselves someday; however, actions, especially a behavioral pattern, show who they truly are, and the habits they have developed are not easily changed. Only a person who is self-aware and committed to growth will change a habit for the goal he or she is shooting for in life.

Additionally, remember that on dating sites, people are marketing themselves and putting only the best information on display. They are not going to say they are stingy in all aspects of their lives. They might not even realize that is an issue.

17

Does He Want to Change You?

Mr. Convert You was a blind date. I had no idea where Anna found these men, but they were coming out of the woodwork. Mr. Convert You had fantastic blue eyes and strawberry-blond hair. At six foot three, he was someone I could look up to—literally. We enjoyed the same music and our local hockey team. At that point, I had been on numerous awful dates. Mr. Convert You seemed to have potential. I took it slow. Really slow.

One night, as we were waiting for our Chinese takeout order we'd called in, he decided to confess something to me. Now, he and I had been seeing each other for a couple of months, and I knew he was into some conspiracy-theory-type stuff. This one took the cake, though. Mr. Convert You believed in lizard people who were in high-ranking positions of political power. We were picking up Chinese food to start our date, and I heard this nonsense from a man who was otherwise intelligent and responsible. One corner of my mouth turned up because I thought, *He has to be kidding.* No, he was not.

When we settled in back at his place, he started telling me about various conspiracy theories. I voiced skepticism. He said, "You'll come around eventually."

This was no red flag on the field; this was more like a red curtain that fell over my vision. After we finished eating, I made an excuse to leave and headed home. I sat in my living room, stunned. I was more annoyed about his desire to change me and my beliefs than about his lizard-people theory.

Look, people believe different things, and I am not going to push my beliefs onto anyone. You make up your own mind. However, for a man to say to me that I need to change is a big fat "No, thanks."

TAKEAWAYS

This is why you need to take things slowly. I was glad we had not gotten physical. Take the time to get to know someone. I am glad he was honest about his beliefs. However, I have no interest in being converted to a belief system. I am happy with who I am. Whoever dates you should be happy with you exactly as he or she finds you.

18

Can He Focus?

The Grillmaster was a sweet person I met in my apartment complex. He had an awesome dog, a cool motorcycle, and a great smile. We would bump into each other at the pool. He made it no secret he was interested from day one. I must admit it was nice for someone to compliment my swimsuit and what was in it.

A group of us often met up at the pool on Saturdays. We would splash, drink, talk, and listen to music. As the day wore on and shifted to twilight, we would all do a potluck. The Grillmaster was a fantastic cook. Many of the others in our group would chip in sides, salads, and condiments, but the Grillmaster and some of the other people would chip in meat for the grill.

The Grillmaster and I had started a little bit of kissy-kissy and flirting. Again, I was in no rush and wanted to know more about him, his children, and his interests before things went deeper. One night, though, the Grillmaster was a little distracted by his phone. As we were sitting next to each other, I caught a glimpse of him sending a photo and message on a dating app to a striking brunette. I wasn't annoyed, because we weren't anything official or serious; however, I was surprised he would message her right in front of me. I did not say anything for a couple of weeks.

We were out for Mexican, when I noticed it again. Finally, when we were alone at his apartment, feeding the dog, I asked what the deal was with his using the dating apps. He was honest. The Grillmaster played a numbers game. He wanted to find someone special, but until that time, the more women he met online, the better his chance of finding someone.

I had seen that brunette. Her photo had not been a "Hey, let's settle down" picture. He was hooking up. I called him out on that, and he, to his credit, was honest again.

"Well, you know a guy has needs. You are the perfect gal to marry. That's why I haven't pushed you into anything— you know, in the bedroom. She is only a bar friend."

I went home and thought about everything he'd said. I wanted a person who was focused and committed.

Even if it was early, as he said, I am the type of woman to settle down with and who deserves a certain level of treatment. In the end, I told him we could be friends only and nothing more. At first, he was okay with the friend status, but then, when he found out I was dating someone new, he went off on me. Interesting double standard.

TAKEAWAYS

Before you date, be clear about your deal breakers and boundaries. You have to know what you are willing to put up with and when it is time to walk away. Although the Grillmaster was honest, something told me to walk away and demand more. I saw his true colors come out once he heard I'd moved on to someone else. They were not pretty, but I have been cursed out before, and I am sure that will not be the last time.

19

Money Can't Buy You Love

A MUTUAL BUSINESS ASSOCIATE WHO WANTED TO PLAY matchmaker introduced me to Mr. Expensive. He was a software engineer for a Fortune 500 company and was nerdy cute. We met about every two weeks downtown for dinner. Expensive and I talked about music, politics, movies, our families, books, and travel. He was funny and witty.

I started to introduce him within my larger friend circle. At first, my friends thought he was great, but one night, they suggested playing games, and Expensive was having none of it. He refused to play. He ended up watching us play because I wanted to play. On the ride home, he criticized my friends. I thought, *No problem. He does not need to be around them.* (Remember the chapter "Your Friends Are Not Dating Him.")

He and I made it to my birthday. He handed me a card after a fabulous dinner at our favorite steakhouse. There was a $300 gift card in it. It was a generous gift.

"I want you to go replace all the kitchen stuff you lost in your divorce," he said.

I was excited, but it felt a little weird. Later, I told my girlfriends about it, and they had reactions of amazement also. When I went to use the gift card, I thought about what he'd said: "replace all the kitchen stuff." I looked at the kitchen stuff in the store and picked up a few things. However, I wanted to spend the money on something else. I fell in love with a painting and eyed a cute bookshelf. Then something heavy fell over my heart.

I was more excited about the painting than the person. Now, if you do not love art, this may be hard to understand, so think of something you see that really moves you and fills you with nothing but happiness. For years, my dogs filled me with happiness, joy, and peace. Or maybe you feel that way about your children or nature.

The gift card led to a realization that I did not have strong feelings for that man. He was fun, and he had a lot going for him, but he was not my person. There was nothing wrong with him. It came down to my heart, which was open and leading me to someone else—someone I could not tell my feelings to yet, because he was not ready. It would have been unfair to keep Expensive as my backup, so I let him go.

TAKEAWAYS

Sometimes it is no one's fault that a relationship does not work out. There does not have to be anything wrong with the other person or you. Do you know how easy it would have been to stay? Cute, nerdy guys with money whom you laugh with are hard to find. However, we didn't match on some level. It was off. Some people call it chemistry; some call it a vibrational level. We simply did not click. I could not imagine a future with him.

In addition, if you give someone a gift, it is that person's gift to do with it what he or she wants. If he'd wanted me to have kitchen stuff, he could have purchased that for me. A gift needs to be without strings. A gift also needs to be in proportion to your relationship. He could afford $300, which was nothing to him, but after my thoughtful $50 gift, the balance felt off.

20

Never Chase

You let others come to you. Never chase! Whether it is a romantic interest, money, or a business opportunity, when you chase, you are showing your desperation. Mr. Smug was gorgeous. I mean, every woman at the country club wanted this guy. One married woman, who was a devote Church of Christ person, said, "I would sin for him." He was kind and attractive, had a full head of hair, and wore great clothing, whether dressy or casual. After bumping into each other several times, we exchanged numbers. He asked me out. I am not going to lie: I was pumped.

I was busy that Friday and Saturday coming up, but we set a date for the following Friday. We then exchanged playful, flirty texting that somehow ended up with me at his house on a Monday night. The banter by text led to a dare. I am headstrong and do not back down from dares. I showed up. Big mistake. I should have waited for Friday.

Never go over to a man's house and chase him and let him know you are interested or, as they say now, thirsty. Play hard to get. We went on our Friday date, but the balance had shifted in the dynamics of how we communicated. He clearly felt he had the advantage. However, that was when things shifted back over to me.

I hate smugness. Good-looking jocks had asked me out over the years, and I never gave them the time of day because of the bravado and smugness. It is not an attractive look on a man. That Friday date was the end for both of us. I told him we were not a great match for each other, and he agreed.

TAKEAWAYS

All relationships have a pace. Some people know they want to get married after a month. God bless. That is not me. I like to get to know someone for two or three months to figure out who he really is. I moved too fast with Smug for my own good, and it bit me on my backside. You need to take the whole person, and that means he or she will have some flaws that drive you crazy and not in a good way.

21

Are Kids Involved?

DATING AT MY AGE MEANS I AM PROBABLY GOING TO meet a majority of people who are divorced with children. Remember, children are always going to come before you. They should. They are dependent on their parents until they are the age of majority, which 99 percent of the time is age eighteen.

I dated several men with children and learned early on that if the children have something going on, that needs to come first. Now, did some men also use their children as an excuse when they needed to rearrange plans or beg off something they did not want to do? Yep! I busted a few men doing that and promptly blocked them when I uncovered it. For example, one man told me he was going to his kids' soccer game, and then I found out later there was no soccer game. In reality, there were a bunch of guys hanging out on the lake, drinking beers, driving Jet Skis, and being stupid enough to post it on Facebook and Instagram.

One night, I was out with a friend at a local hangout. There was a gorgeous man at the table near us, and I could have sworn I caught him looking at me a few times. He had the light artic-blue eyes I go nuts for, regardless of if he was bald or not. From what I could tell, he was with his sister, brother-in-law, and nieces and nephews.

Feeling brave, I asked the server for a pen. After he exited the restroom, when he passed my table, I gave him my number. I told him, "I never do this," which was true, "but I had to take a shot."

He politely told me he was there with his daughter.

"Say no more. I get it. You are out with your daughter; that is special time, and you do not get those years back."

However, for any Romeo who lied about spending time with his children in order to hang with the boys, there was a reason I ghosted: the dishonesty.

One man, Weekend Father, had a grown daughter with her own children and a son in college who lived with him every other weekend. His son made no bones about the fact that he did not like me. It didn't matter why to me; it was clear he was uncomfortable with my being around.

One night, Weekend Father and I were eating pizza and watching a movie on the couch. His son came in with his girlfriend and said, "Ew, Dad, what are you doing?" We were only sitting on the couch, watching a movie, with an open pizza box in front of us. Obviously, nothing was going on when they walked in, but his son's mind went straight to other stuff.

After a few dates, I told Weekend Father, "Listen, if your son is uncomfortable with my being around, you are welcome to come to my place or invite me over when he is not home that weekend. I understand how awkward it could be for children to think of their parents being romantic with someone new."

Oddly, his ex-wife had remarried. Maybe that was the issue. Maybe his son did not want to have to worry about a new stepparent being in the mix. Regardless, the relationship did not work out for other reasons.

TAKEAWAYS

If you are dating someone with children, realize you will always come second. That is it. There's no need to complicate this. Those children should be a priority too. Do you really want to be with someone who doesn't make his or her children a priority?

However, watch out for liars who use their children—or any family or friends—as their escape hatch to get out of plans with you. If only a liar's pants actually did catch on fire with every lie.

22

Background Checks Needed

Mr. Criminal Record met me on an online social media app and struck up a conversation. Remember that people online can pretend to be anyone. There are bad people out there. You cannot trust everyone! People need to earn your trust.

Criminal Record told me he had an amazing job and a great relationship with his adult son and boasted of military experience. I picked Criminal Record up at work one day and met his adult son. While Criminal Record went to close out some computer stuff, I asked his son for dirt about his dad in a playful way. His son, without missing a beat, said, "I have only known him for a year. My mom raised me."

By then, Criminal Record was back and ready to go, so I put on my best poker face and let those words sink in. Criminal Record had made himself sound like father of the year. He sounded too good to be true, and something felt off.

I started digging. After doing a background check, I found he had a domestic violence conviction in another state. I decided to ask him about it.

Criminal Record gave his side of the story, but at that point, the damage was done. At the beginning of the relationship, during our long chats, he could have brought up his past. Instead, I had to go find out the truth, and what he'd told me did not match up.

Always background-check the people you date. I have had female clients who dated and even married men without ever doing a deep dive into their background. They find out in horror later that there is a list of felony charges the men forgot to mention prior to the wedding. Please go in with eyes wide open. Protect yourself.

TAKEAWAYS

A background check is cheaper than damaged credit, a hospital bill for broken ribs, or a divorce from a con artist. Know whom you are really dealing with, and do not project onto this new prospect what you want to see. See what is really there, and if something doesn't ring true, listen to your gut.

In addition, if you are a parent, your children will be around this person, and in a future custody fight, a criminal record could matter. Any issues with drugs, alcohol, sex charges, domestic violence, or assault are fair play in a custody fight.

23

Can He Show Empathy?

THERE WAS A MAN I HAD BEEN SEEING ON AND OFF FOR a year. We must have been on more than twenty-five or thirty dates. Like the Taylor Swift song "We Are Never Ever Getting Back Together," we would end the relationship and then wander back into each other's life. There were so many red flags that I listed them and then stopped counting at twenty.

He never wanted to call me a girlfriend. He said he didn't want a relationship, but he enjoyed relationship perks. He introduced me as "Loretta. She's a lawyer," or he wouldn't introduce me at all. I met one of his friends from high school one time for dinner. I got drunk-dialed a few times. Most of my friends, after the fifth breakup, were sick of hearing his name. I was too, so I will not even give a name. Eventually, Mr. Nameless and I settled into being just friends, but he still wanted perks. We would spend time hanging out at either his house or mine.

At one point, I had some scary symptoms and went to the doctor. The doctor did a biopsy, and I got a bad diagnosis. I contacted my friends, including him. Mr. Nameless said by text, "I'm sorry. At least it is treatable." He spent that day and the rest of that week complaining about his job. Actually, he complained about his job regularly. When we spoke that week, every conversation was about his horrible, demanding job. Mr. Nameless did not mention my diagnosis, let alone offer help, support, or a shoulder to cry on.

All my other friends, male friends included, from work and church checked on me regularly. They offered support. They listened to me cry. They said, "You are going to be okay. Let us know if you need help. We mean it." Crickets from Mr. Nameless, who'd insisted, "We are not in a relationship, but we are friends." Worst friend ever.

TAKEAWAYS

If a man cannot show empathy or support you in a major time of need, get rid of him. You deserve someone who will show up for you. I saw behavior I did not like, and I made excuses. I started expecting less and less from this man, until we were so-called friends.

He did not even know how to be a friend, and that was when I exited stage right.

24

Keep Your Money in Your Wallet

THE FIRST PERSON I DATED AFTER MY DIVORCE WAS final was a setup. My friend Anna told me she wanted to introduce me to a guy. She told me he was smart, was a CPA, and had adopted a child with his ex-wife. He was Anna's stepson's baseball coach.

I took a deep breath and thought, *When was the last time I had a kiss?* I had been unhappy for so long before my divorce that such a simple act, which most couples do without even considering the meaning behind it, was foreign to me. Had it been three years? *No, wait—four!* I smiled and shrugged. *Batter up. Why not? If I hate him, then no harm done. If I like him, then I can dip my toe into dating again after an almost twenty-five-year hiatus.*

The venue Anna selected was her country club, where a drink was twenty dollars, a salad was fifteen dollars without protein, and the special grouper of the day was thirty-six dollars. *These are stupid, crazy prices for people making well into six figures, and my groceries for the week cost less*, I thought. However, it was Wednesday at the club, which meant that everything was supposed to be half off—in other words, normal restaurant prices.

As I stood at our table and talked to Anna and her husband, Derek, she told me, "Bright Eyes is here."

I turned my head and noticed his amazing eyes matched the bright aqua color of his shirt. He was tall, dark-haired, and broad-shouldered. If I have a type, that is my physical type. Every mistake I'd made in my twenties looked like this man. As I gazed and smiled, Anna whispered in my ear, "I dated him before I met my husband."

Wait—what? I thought.

Bright Eyes walked over and introduced himself.

The group made small talk. We ordered and received our drinks. Our table of eight consisted of all couples. When Bright Eyes was busy talking to the person to his right, I turned to my left and whispered to Anna, "What the hell do you mean you dated him? I thought he was Brian's coach."

Anna nodded and sipped. "He is."

Bright Eyes asked me a question. I turned and politely answered. I was interested, but I noticed a few things.

First, he was not talking much to me. He seemed to be hitting it off more with the couple next to him. Another male at the table asked him what he did for a living. He was not a CPA anymore but had a high-level job at a major employer in our area. We ate. We drank. We ordered and shared dessert. The bill arrived.

The server, realizing we were coupled up at the table, gave the men the tickets. The men checked the bills. There was no half-price discount; everything was full price. Anna talked to the manager of the country club, who explained that the policy had changed.

Bright Eyes had just met me. I think we both had sticker shock. The bill could easily have bought me a month's worth of groceries. I offered to pay half, and he accepted. Now I was a bit surprised. I'd expected him to say, "Oh no, I couldn't," but he did not. The waitperson took our bill back and split it.

I guess he is not interested, I thought, *and he is not a gentleman*. I paid my half and left.

As I was driving home, my phone rang. I pushed the hands-free button, and it was Grace, one of my friends who had been at dinner. "What did you think?" she asked.

"He didn't pay for me," I complained.

"Well, it was a meetup, not a date. Maybe he was nervous."

Call waiting beeped.

Anna, who had set us up, asked, "So what did you think?"

"We split the check."

"Oh, that doesn't mean anything. He asked for your number. Can I give it to him?"

I thought about those eyes and the moment I first had seen him, when the hair on the back of my neck had gone up. Besides, it had been years since a man had touched me. "Sure, Anna, give him my number," I said right before I went down the rabbit hole for my adventure.

TAKEAWAYS

Ladies, do not offer to pay. Seriously, until the pay gap is rectified, do not pay when a man takes you out. Bright Eyes was established in his career and made more money than I did. I was in the middle of starting my life over after the divorce. I had tons of start-up expenses. However, I also wanted to make it clear that I was not expecting anything from him. In his brain, the extravagant bill was probably a nonevent. To a struggling newly single female entrepreneur in a male-dominated profession, it was my month's grocery bill.

The other error I made was in not asking enough questions before the meetup. Before you get set up, get all the dirt possible on the person. I started Googling and background-checking people after that date.

I cornered Anna later to get the full scoop on Bright Eyes. "How long did you date? What did you do? Why didn't you want him?" I needed more information up front on this person. More details from Anna beforehand would have saved me some aggravating encounters.

Also, you need to keep a clear head and focus on what is in front of you and not what you want to be there. He reminded me of someone from my past, and I unknowingly projected things onto him. I also had a false backstory and made assumptions based on what my friend had told me. Avoid making assumptions based on others' looks, their jobs, and the stories they tell. Once again, because he worked with children, I thought that meant he had compassion and similar values. This conclusion probably happened in nanoseconds because of how the human brain processes things and makes assessments based on past experiences.

Finally, do not put yourself on the meat market until you are ready. My friends meant well, but I was not mentally prepared to date again. Yes, my divorce was final, and yes, the marriage had been dead for years before the divorce finally happened. However, I had not dealt with any of my baggage. If you have not worked on yourself yet and cleared out all those old negative beliefs, you will carry them into a new relationship. That is not fair to either person and could destroy something that has real potential.

25

The Epiphany

WHAT DID I LEARN AFTER A YEAR OF DATING? I LEARNED to say no to men and yes to myself. I realized I was attracting the wrong men. I needed to get clearer in terms of what I wanted, what my deal breakers were, and what my boundaries were. That meant turning inward and figuring out who I was, what standards I had, and what was negotiable.

I realized I had some incorrect beliefs about relationships and myself. For example, from the earliest moment I can remember, my family and culture told me a woman's sole purpose was to get married and have children. I was told if I did not accomplish those two milestones, I was a failure. I had some hard lessons to learn and difficult realizations to make about myself. It humbled me. I had to admit I did not have clear boundaries. I tried to build the plane while flying. My plan was always to be single and work on myself in the year after the divorce was final; I did not listen to myself, though. I had a good plan, and I did not stick with it. I gave in when my well-meaning friends gave me advice, instead of listening to my own intuition.

In fact, repeatedly, as you can see, I did not follow my intuition. I put myself in danger. Future *Dateline* Story could have been a serial killer, but I didn't know any of the other men either. Even the ones I was set up with through mutual friends had their own false beliefs and agendas. The dating apps allow anything and do not mark or flag people. I saw a news story about several women who were raped by the same man who had an online dating profile.

I talked myself out of boundaries. I let people in too soon. I trusted the wrong people. There are skilled liars out there who take pride on how many dates they can fool and juggle at the same time. STDs and STIs do not discriminate in terms of who gets them. All one good person needs is a skilled liar with pretty eyes to undue a clean health record. I needed to realize that when someone told me or showed me his true self, it was okay to walk away and not make excuses for bad behavior. People will say, I love you, to manipulate. I was like a child walking into a den of wolves while covered in fresh blood. I was not prepared.

I needed to say yes to myself. Yes, I need to be left alone longer. Yes, I need self-care. Yes, I can buy my own dinner, my own diamonds, and my own damn home. Yes, I can show up as my authentic self. If someone doesn't like it, he can go out the door he came in. Finally, I realized I did not need to impress these men.

These dates needed to impress me. These dates needed to prove to me that they were worthy of my time and attention. Because if a man is not worth my time, I can spend my energy on other fun, productive, and enriching activities. I can stay home and do self-care on Saturday night. I do not need to be out on a date. I do not need to pair up. I can be happily single instead of unhappily married. Please join me. We are the cool table.

If you enjoyed this book, please give it a review.
Also, check out my website, www.legallyquirky.com,
for my blog and life-coaching packages.

Printed in the United States
by Baker & Taylor Publisher Services